OVERSIZE

BEN LOMOND
COMMUNITY
LIBRARY

OVERSIZE
J
629.422 COPY 4
F Freeman, Mae (Blacker)
Space base. c1972. 4.75

BEN LOMOND
COMMUNITY
LIBRARY
DISCARD

SPACE BASE

FRANKLIN WATTS, INC.
New York, 1972

SPACE BASE

J 629.422 F
COPY 4

BY MAE FREEMAN
Illustrated by Raul Mina Mora

SANTA CRUZ PUBLIC LIBRARY
SANTA CRUZ, CALIFORNIA

SBN 531-02029-0
Library of Congress Catalog Card Number: 71-182290
Copyright © 1972 by Mae Freeman
Printed in the United States of America

SPACE BASE

The rocket stands on its launching pad, ready for blast-off. Inside the rocket, you lie on your couch, straps on tight. The two astronauts are ready, too. But they are not as excited as you are. They take this trip often.

Suddenly there is a great flash from the engines, and a roar like thunder. You feel your body being pressed down on the couch.

The rocket zooms upward, going faster and faster. It curves over slowly as it goes up. Through a window you can see the earth. It seems to be dropping away from your rocket.

The day was bright when you were on the ground, but now it is getting dark very quickly. The blue sky is changing to deep purple. Very soon the sky is as black as night and full of shining stars. You are out in space!

Now you notice a small, bright dot up ahead. It looks like a star, but it is much brighter. The dot is moving slowly along while the stars seem to be standing still.

The bright dot gets bigger and bigger. As you come near, you can see that it is a huge wheel. And the wheel keeps turning —slowly, slowly.

The wheel is a Space Base, and you are on your way to visit it. The rocket that is taking you there is called a shuttle. The whole trip in the shuttle, from earth to Space Base, takes only 15 minutes.

For now, you can only imagine this exciting trip, because there is no base out in space yet. But scientists are working on plans. Before too long, there is sure to be one base up there, and maybe even two or three. Shuttles will go back and forth carrying people and supplies.

Meanwhile, in this book you can read about Space Bases and find out how interesting it will be to visit one.

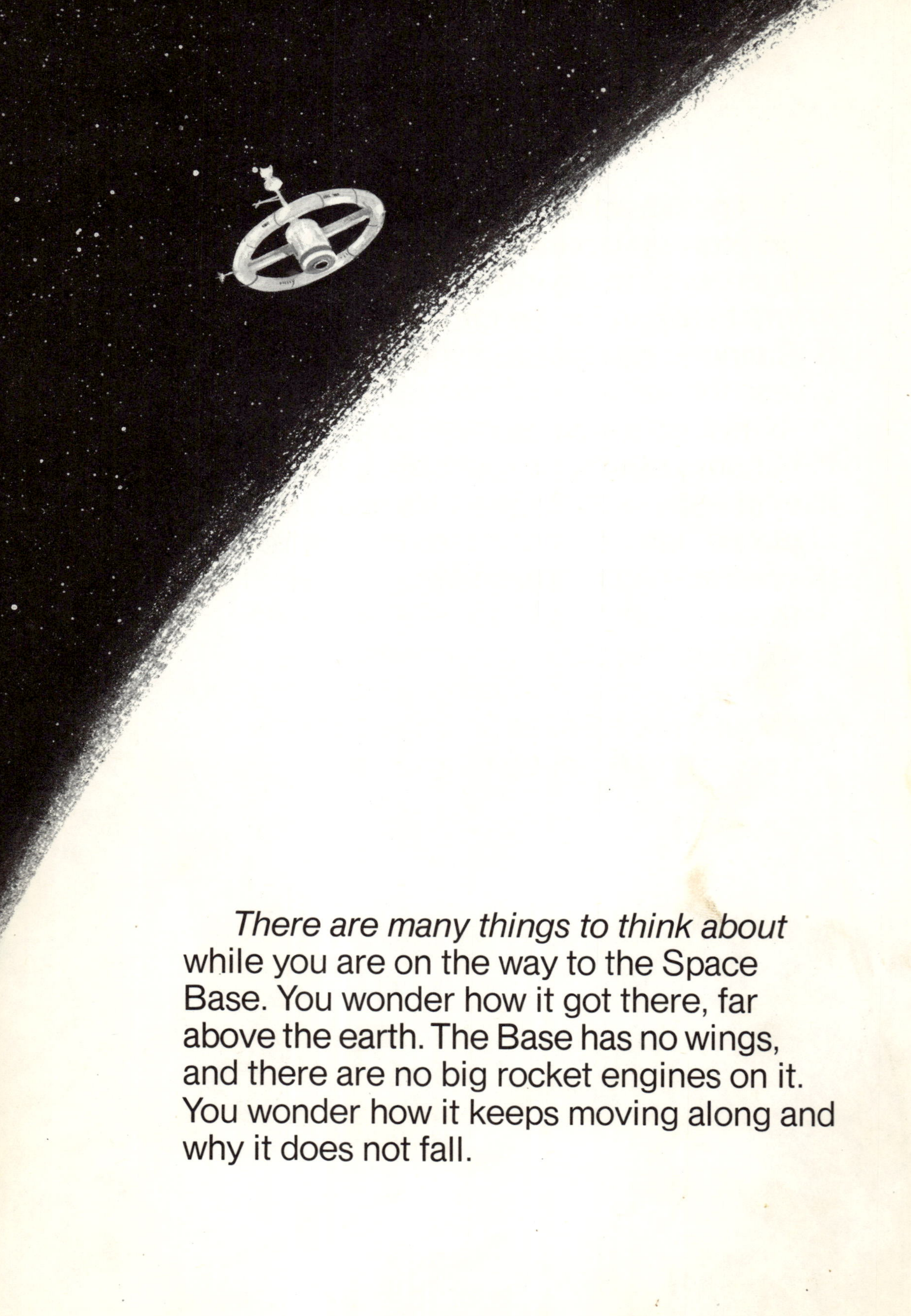

There are many things to think about while you are on the way to the Space Base. You wonder how it got there, far above the earth. The Base has no wings, and there are no big rocket engines on it. You wonder how it keeps moving along and why it does not fall.

Long ago, a famous scientist named Isaac Newton became interested in why things fall. One day he saw an apple drop from a tree and hit the ground with a thump. It reminded him that all things fall downward unless they are somehow kept from falling.

Newton thought about it for a long time. He figured out that it must be the earth itself that pulls everything toward it. His idea was right. And this kind of pulling power was named gravity.

It is gravity that pulls your body downward so that you stay on the ground. If you jump off a fence, gravity quickly pulls you downward. Because of the pull of gravity, tables and chairs rest on the floor. Books stay on the shelf. Water pours downward. Without gravity, everything—even water—would float around in the air.

It is gravity that pulls a ball downward when it drops out of your hand. Think of what would happen without gravity. The ball would stay there, floating around right next to your hand.

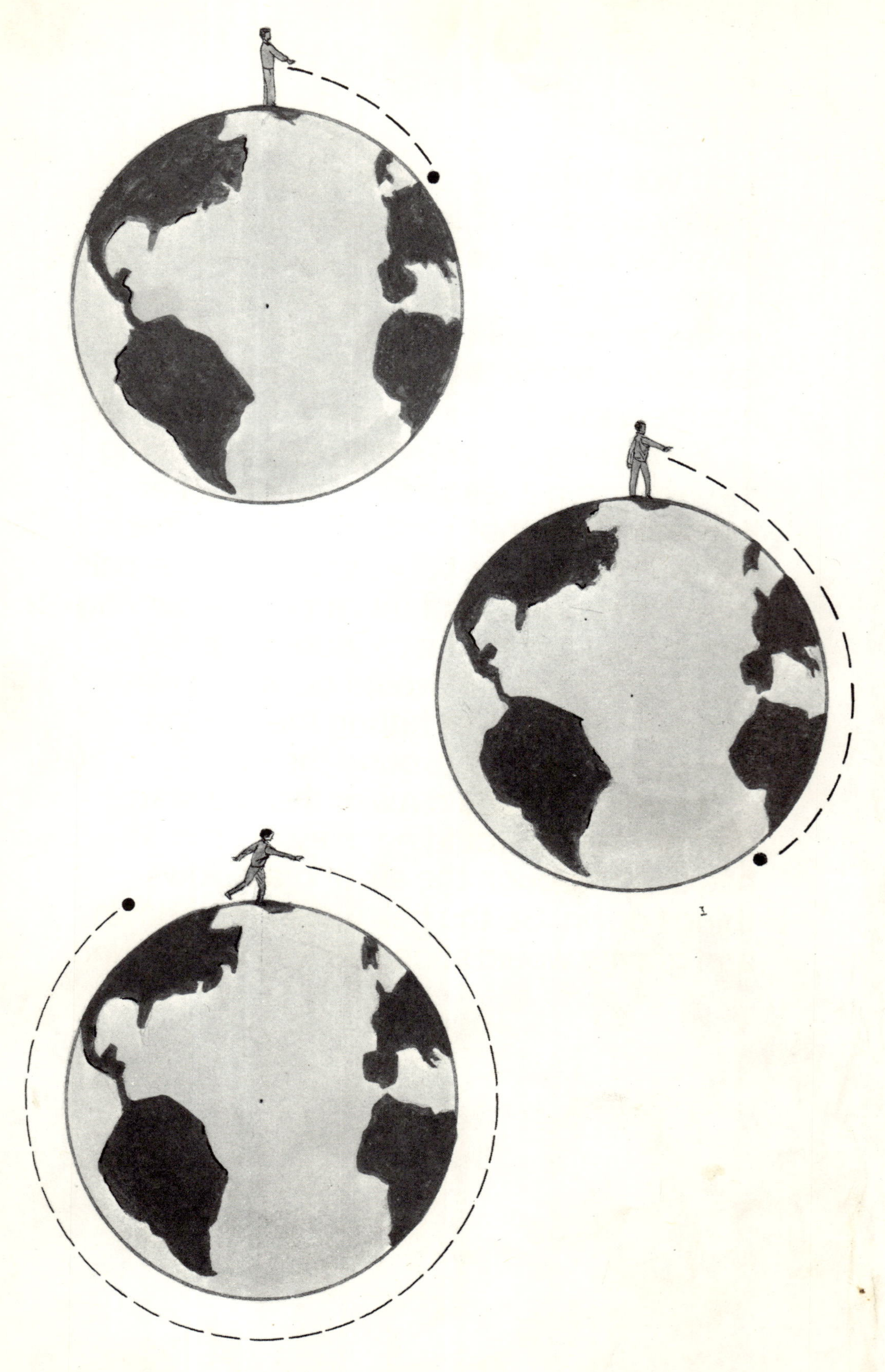

If you throw the ball straight ahead, gravity still pulls it downward. But you gave the ball a push when you threw it, so it does not fall to the ground at once. It moves ahead while it falls. The harder and faster you throw the ball, the farther away it hits the ground.

Suppose you had some way of making the ball zoom ahead much, much faster than a bullet—thousands of miles an hour. The pull of gravity would still make the ball curve downward. But this time, the curving path would just fit the roundness of the earth. Then the ball would go all the way around without ever hitting the ground. It would be in orbit around the earth.

Even if you could make the ball start out that fast, it would not stay in orbit. It has to go through the air, and air slows things down. So the ball would slow down, and gravity would soon pull it to the ground.

Far above the earth there is no air to slow things down. That is why the Space Base was put into orbit 300 miles high. It did not go up all in one piece. It was put together up there from many parts. Each part was boosted into space and put into orbit by rockets.

All the parts, going about 18,000 miles an hour, stayed in orbit side by side. Then workmen came up in shuttles and put the parts together in the shape of a wheel. Small rockets were fired to set the wheel turning slowly.

And there it is, far above the earth, a bright ring in the black sky.

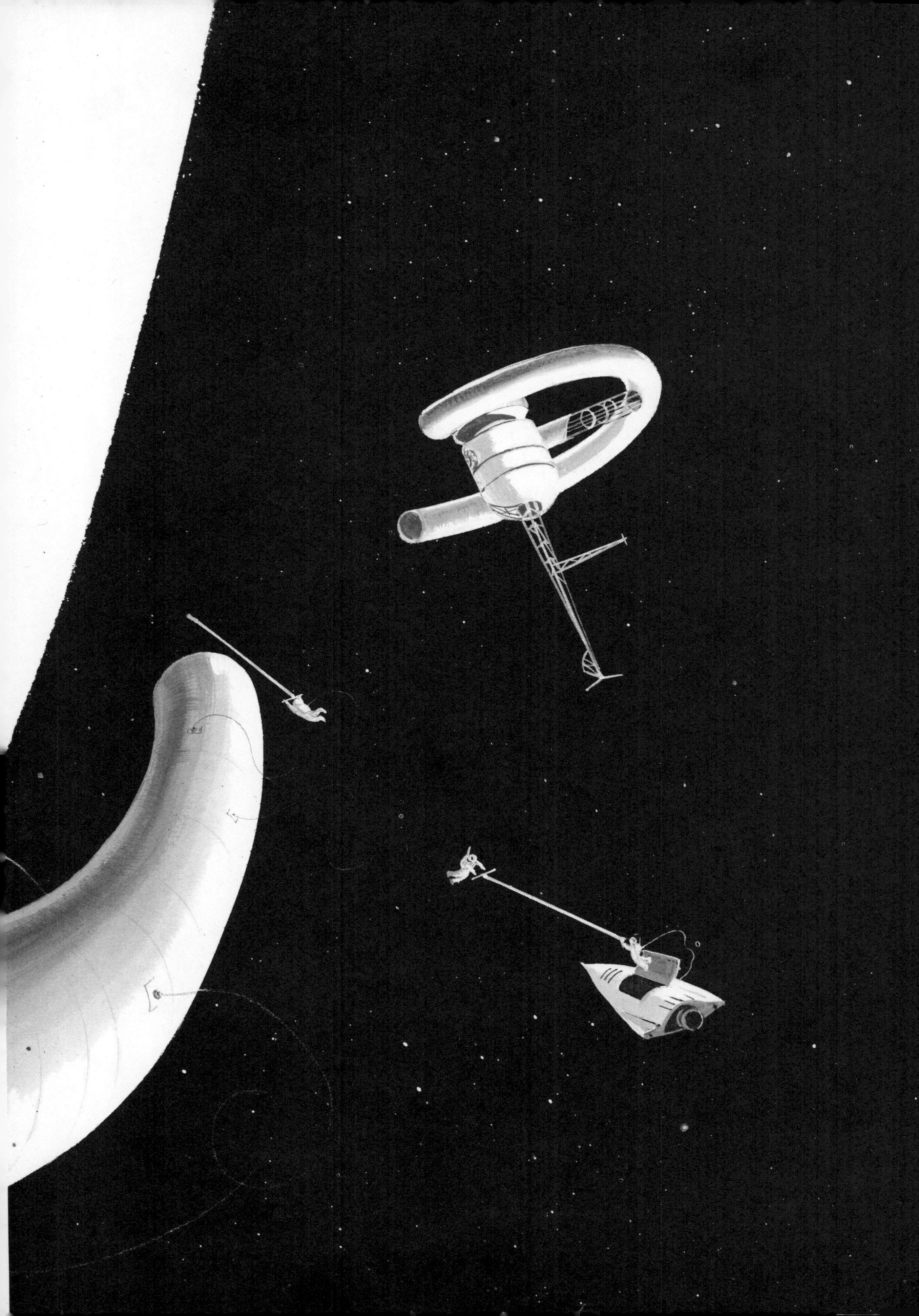

Your shuttle gets nearer and nearer to the Space Base. Very soon the huge wheel is just above you, and you can see a round opening in the center. Two men wearing space suits are there, holding on to a railing. They are part of the crew of the Space Base.

The men reach out and help the shuttle slide into the opening. There is a little bump as the shuttle locks in tightly.

Now you are ready to go into the Base. The pilot astronaut warns you that you are now weightless. He tells you to open the straps of the couch. And then you find out what he means when he says you are weightless.

You start to get up. Instead of standing on your feet, you find yourself floating. And nothing is holding you up! You feel as light as a feather—you seem to weigh nothing at all. Now you are really a spaceman.

You have to keep remembering that things are different in space. All your life on earth you have been held down by gravity. And now, in space, you do not feel any pull—you float wherever you happen to be.

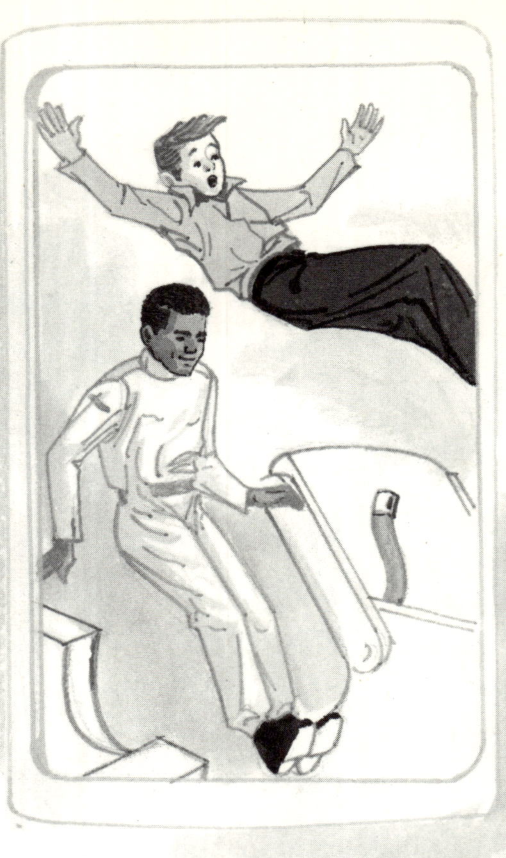

Follow the pilot. He gives himself a little push from his couch and goes floating to the door. Give yourself a little push, too. You are not very good at it. You bump against the walls a few times before you get to the door.

The men help you as you leave the shuttle. They boost you into a tunnel that has a ladder along the side. The tunnel goes from the center to the rim of the wheel.

You move backward along the ladder, putting hand after hand and foot after foot. And then you notice something strange. You are beginning to lose the feeling of floating. With each step, you have to hold on a little tighter.

At the end of the ladder, you step down onto a floor. Just a minute ago, you were floating around. And now, here you are, walking again! How did it happen?

SANTA CRUZ PUBLIC LIBRARY
SANTA CRUZ, CALIFORNIA

The main part of the Space Base is a circle of long, narrow rooms. And the circle keeps turning, like a wheel.

The turning makes things push outward. On earth, you can notice this kind of push when you are riding in a car. If the car makes a sharp turn to one side, the turning makes you lean to the opposite side. It feels as if something is actually pushing you.

That is how the turning of the Space Base pushes your body outward and makes a kind of artificial gravity. Your feet press against the rim of the wheel, and this makes you feel as if you are standing on a floor.

In space, there is no "up" and there is no "down." In a Space Base that is turning, "up" is toward the center of the wheel and "down" is toward the rim.

The drawing shows what happens when the Base turns and pushes people outward. Notice that "down" is different for each person. It depends on where he is in the circle.

The center part of the Base moves around too slowly to form any artificial gravity. This part is called the hub. Everything inside the hub is weightless.

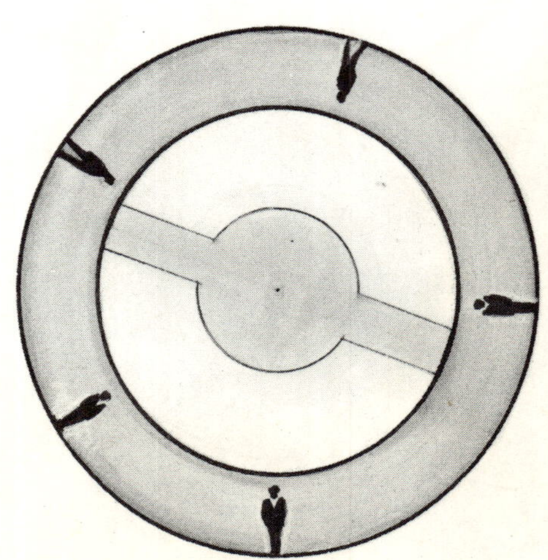

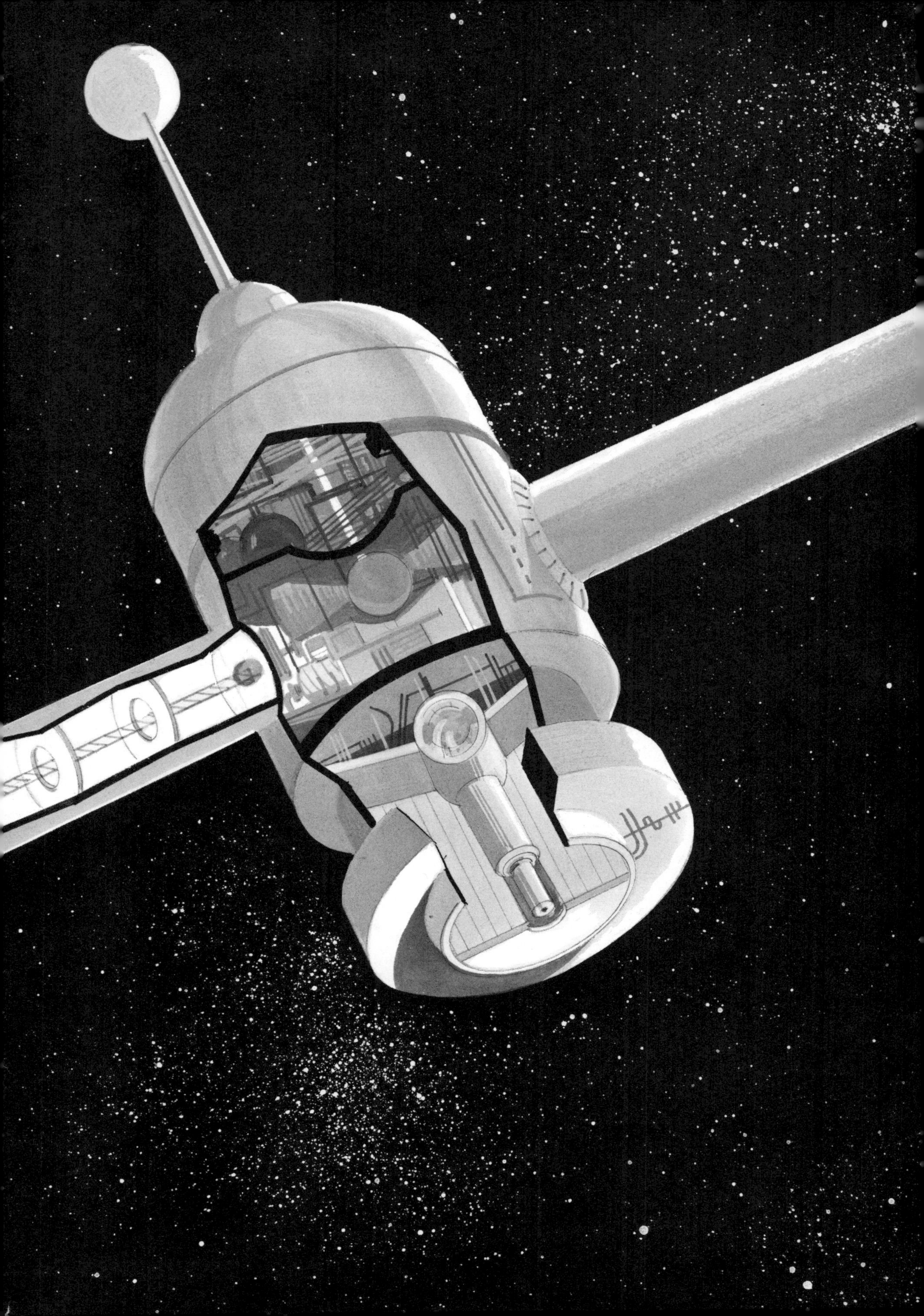

Even though there is no air so high above the earth, there is plenty of it inside the Space Base. It is brought up in supply shuttles. This is not too hard to do, because air can be cooled and squeezed tightly until it becomes a liquid. Then it takes up much less room in the tanks. In space science, liquid oxygen is called LOX. LOX gives the people on the Base enough air for comfortable living.

It is not as easy to keep enough water handy. Water is very heavy and takes up a lot of room. But there are ways to use water over and over. Every drop is saved, no matter what it has been used for. Then it is made pure and clean again with chemicals.

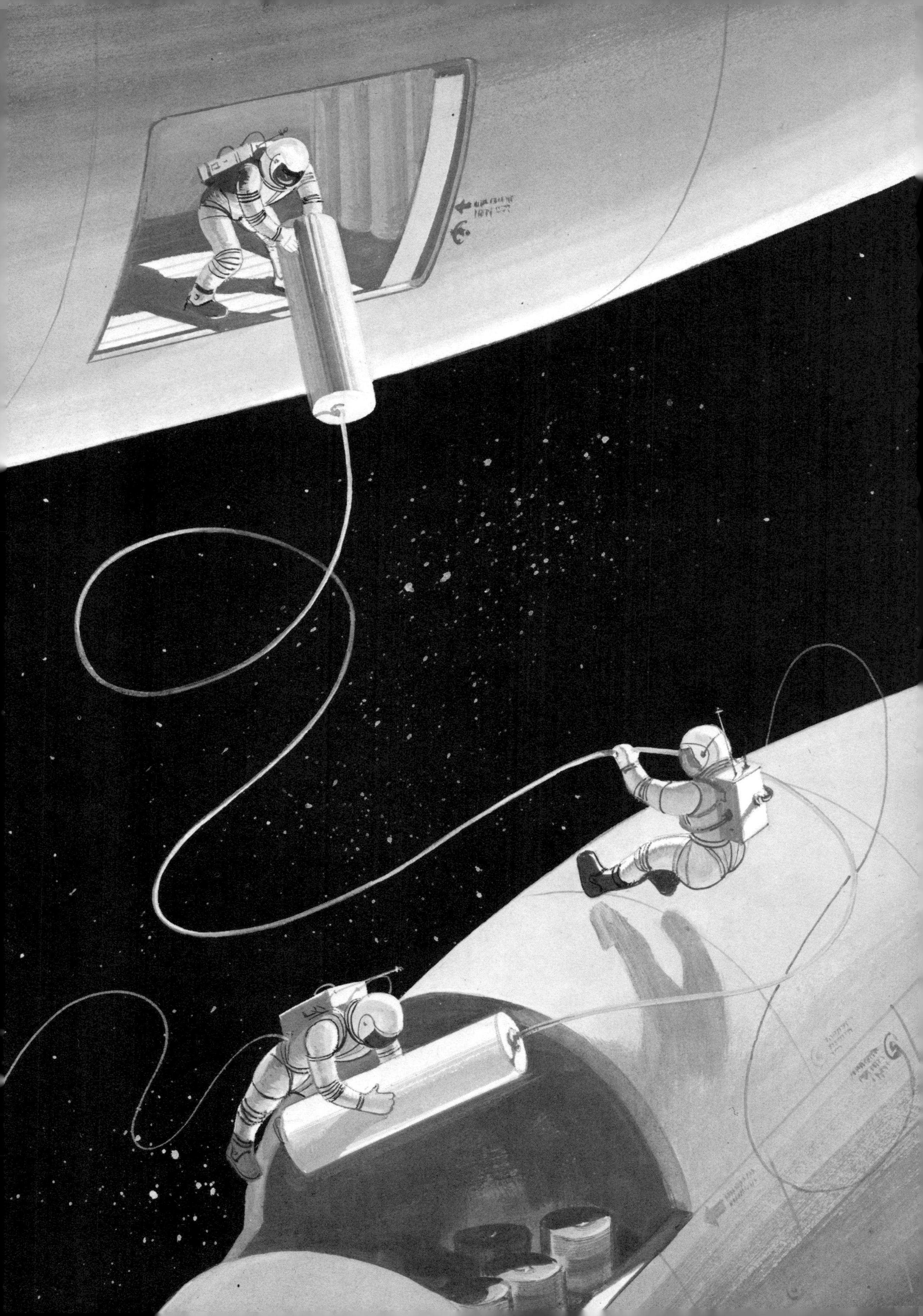

Most of the power needed to keep the Base running comes from an atomic reactor. All atomic reactors send out harmful rays, so this one is set on a tall tower that stands out from the hub. This puts it at a safe distance from the people on the Base.

Inside the Base, the engine room is a busy place. It is crowded with all kinds of machines that hum and clatter. There are motors and pumps and air conditioners. There are chemical tanks and tubes for making the air and water pure.

One of the rooms in the Base has bunk beds along the walls. In space there is no regular day-and-night way of living. The men take turns sleeping and working, so there are usually some people asleep in the bunk room.

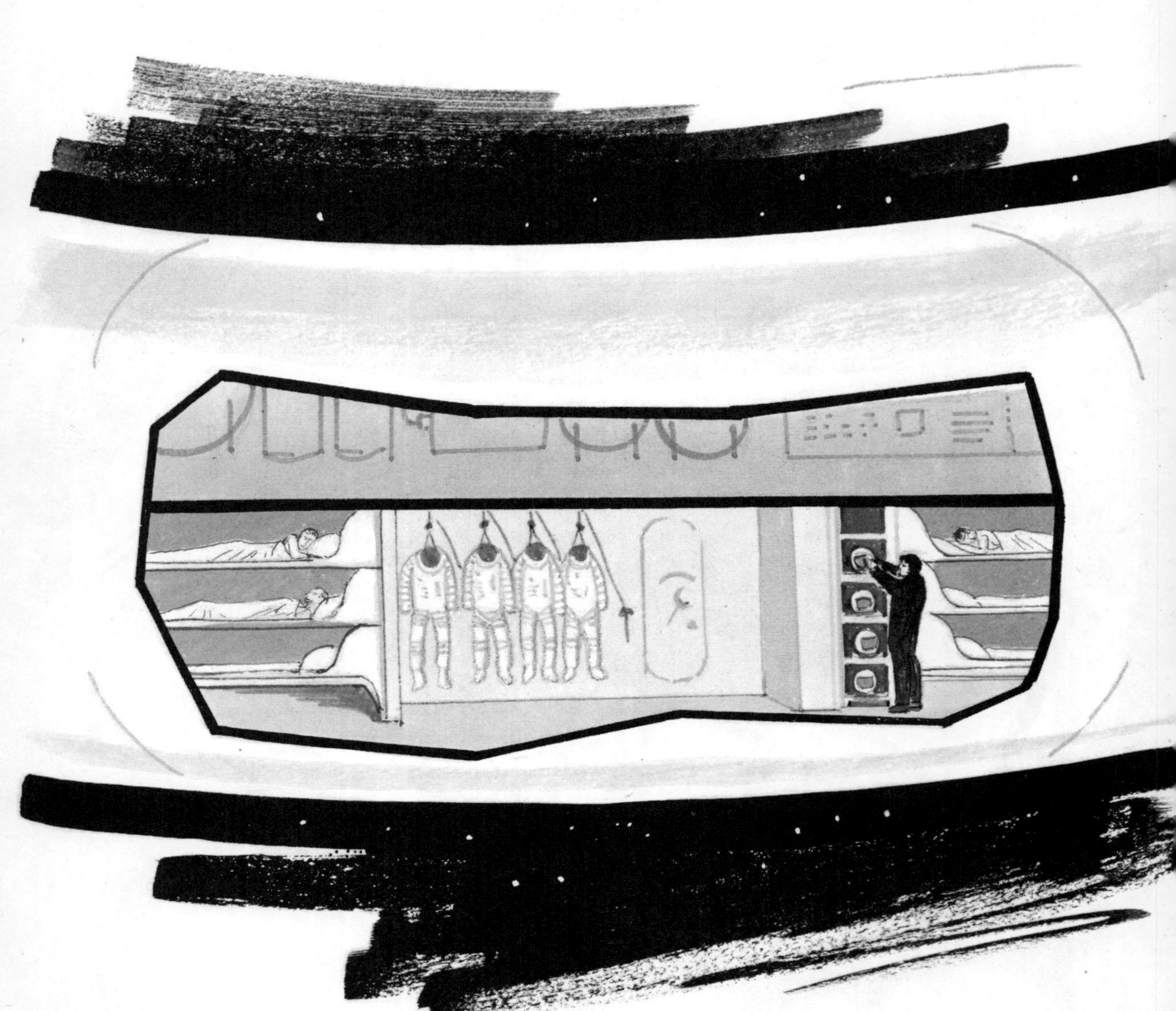

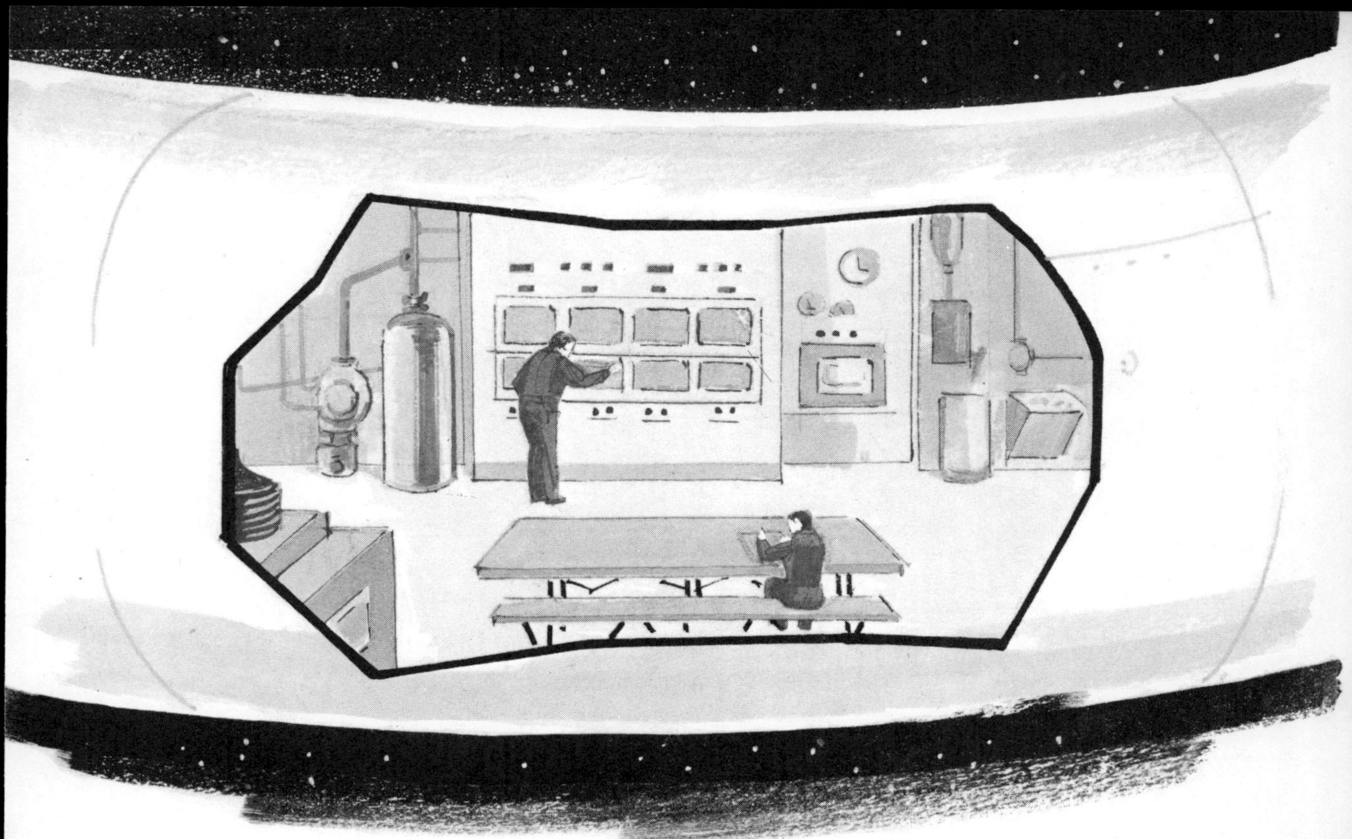

Next to the bunk room there is a kitchen with a long table in the center. Frozen food is brought up to the Base in the shuttles and kept in refrigerators. It takes only a few minutes to heat a package dinner in a special oven.

On earth, food can be cooked in open pots and pans. But in the Base this would put too much steam into the air through all the rooms. And it would be very hard to get rid of the cooking smells.

Garbage, wastepaper, and all other used-up materials are not dumped out into space. They must all be taken back to earth in the shuttle.

Each person on the Space Base has a special job to do. Everyone keeps so busy that the workrooms are usually very quiet. So it is surprising to hear loud noises coming from one of the rooms—squawks and barks and chirps and squeals. It sounds like a farmyard or a circus.

Mice, rabbits, chickens, and insects of many kinds are kept here. Scientists want to see if animals living in space grow up the same as animals on earth.

Two small monkeys live in the hub, where they are weightless. They get the best of care to keep them healthy. Scientists check the monkeys often to see how they are getting along, living for most of their lives without gravity.

In the astronomy room, a scientist is working with some star pictures that were taken with a camera-telescope. This telescope is not in the Space Base. It is outside, on a little space station of its own, where it is clear of any shaking from the machinery on the big Base. Besides, the Base is turning, so it would be hard to keep the telescope pointed at a certain star or planet.

The camera-telescope is several hundred feet away, moving in the same orbit as the Space Base. This means that someone must go out there to bring back the pictures. An astronomer does this by taking a space walk. He puts on his space suit and goes into a little room called an air lock. The air is pumped out. Then he opens the outside door and steps into space.

The astronomer is going to the telescope, so he points a gas pistol in exactly the opposite direction. The pistol works like a very small rocket engine. It shoots out a little puff of gas and gives the astronomer a push toward the telescope. He floats over to it, trailing a long safety line from the Base.

When the astronomer gets to the telescope, he takes the film out of the camera and puts in new film. Then he can set the camera to take pictures by itself. Or, if he wants to, he can control the camera by radio from the astronomy room. When his work is done, the astronomer uses his gas pistol to get back to the Base.

Pictures of stars are sharp and clear when they are taken in space this way. That is because the light from the stars does not have to go through many miles of air on its way to the camera.

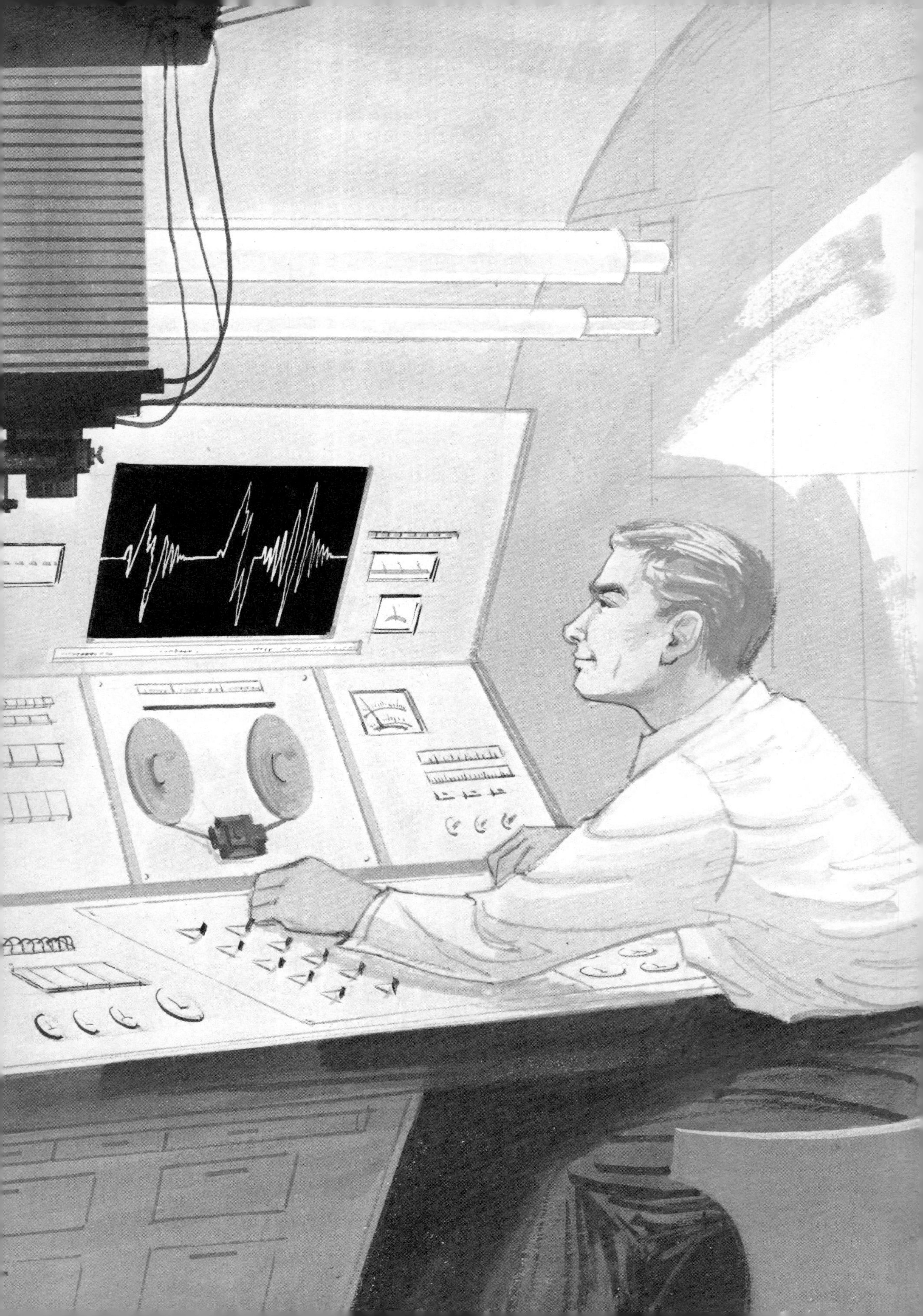

In a corner of the astronomy room, another scientist is working at his desk. He is checking over some long strips of paper with strange-looking marks on them. These marks are measurements of cosmic rays that come from everywhere in space.

Cosmic rays are not like light rays. They are streams of tiny parts of atoms that zoom through space. No one knows where they come from or what gives them their terrific speed.

When these mysterious rays come through the air, the measurements are not very clear. That is why scientists hope to find out more about cosmic rays by measuring them in space, before they hit the air.

In the recreation room, people can throw darts or play cards and other games. The TV brings in shows from earth, and music is usually coming from the hi-fi.

This room is bright and cheerful. It has two large windows, one on each side. It is a good place to rest for a while and take a look outside the Space Base.

From one of the windows, you can see only black sky. Out here, the sky is always black and never changes color. It is speckled all over with bright dots that are the stars and planets.

The sky did not look like this when you were on the ground. In the daytime, it was usually bright blue. Even at night, the sky never looked as dark as this.

The sky looks black now because you are 300 miles out in space. You are above the layer of air that is all around the earth. And it is the air that changes the way things look when you are on the ground. When light from the sun goes through hundreds of miles of air, the rays spread out all around. This lights up everything on earth more evenly. It also makes the sky look bright.

On earth at night, even the weak light from the moon and stars is spread out by the air. So the night sky never looks quite as inky black as the sky looks when you are in space.

Now go to the window on the other side of the room, where you can see the earth. There are white patches on it here and there. The patches are clouds. The oceans look dark green, and the ground is brown and wrinkled. The wrinkles are really high mountains.

You are so far away from the earth that it looks like a painted map. But you know very well that many things are going on down there. Millions of people are moving around, working and playing. Cars are speeding down long, white highways. Huge planes are taking off and flying through the air.

But you can see none of this. From where you are, the earth is only a beautiful colored map. And the map is changing slowly, even while you watch, because you are moving along over it. It is hard to believe that you are going almost 18,000 miles an hour! The Space Base takes only about an hour and a half to make each trip around the earth.

Notice a small round window overhead. If you look up through it, you can see the hub. Something interesting is happening there right now. A rocket is ready to leave for the moon.

The rocket is still locked into the opening. But as you watch, it begins to back up and drift slowly away from the hub.

When the rocket is clear of the Base, it blasts off, trailing an orange-red flame behind it. In a few moments it is only a bright speck far off in the black sky. Soon it disappears altogether. The rocket is well on its way to the moon, carrying men and supplies from the Space Base.

This rocket goes to the moon. Someday, there may be rockets that carry people to Mars or one of the other planets. All these trips become easier if they start out from space instead of from the ground. The huge, turning ring is named just right, for it is truly a base in space.

It takes many years of planning and testing to put a Space Base into orbit. Before this can be done, much smaller space stations will be sent up.

A small space station can be made from the fuel tank of a moon rocket. That is one of the parts that falls away when the fuel is used up. The tank could be put into orbit around the earth and then fitted out as an orbiting workshop. Several men could work there at the same time, doing different kinds of experiments. They will be weightless because there will be no gravity of any kind.

Later, the first large station will be put together. It could also be made of used-up parts of moon rockets. There will be a crew of about twelve people. This space station will be a stopping-over place for trips to the moon. It will have a turning motion, so it will be the first station to have artificial gravity.

As more workshops and space stations are put into orbit, engineers will find out the best ways to build and run them. Then everything will be ready for building the big Space Base that you have been reading about in this book. Perhaps by that time you will be ready to sign on as one of the crew.

ABOUT THE AUTHOR

Mae Freeman is a native of Chicago, Illinois, and a graduate of the University of Chicago. She has written many books for children, mainly in the field of science. She now lives in Bound Brook, New Jersey.